# A Saviour is Born

for the Black Man and Woman of America

## The Honorable Minister Louis Farrakhan

Copyright © 2022 The Final Call Foundation

All rights reserved.

ISBN: 979-8-9859218-5-4

# DEDICATION

The Honorable Minister Louis Farrakhan delivered this lecture on February 22, 1981, at the Auditorium Theatre in Chicago, Illinois, marking the first commemoration of Saviours' Day under his leadership of the Nation of Islam.

Saviours' Day is an annual commemoration of the birth of Master Fard Muhammad, the Great Mahdi of the Muslims and the long-awaited Messiah of the Christians, who appeared in North America on July 4, 1930.

He was born on February 26, 1877 in the Holy City of Mecca.

The observance was first established by the Most Honorable Elijah Muhammad as Saviour's Day (singular) but the Honorable Minister Louis Farrakhan elevated it to a plural commemoration (Saviours') to honor the growth in divinity of the Honorable Elijah Muhammad.

The Most Honorable Elijah Muhammad was born on October 7, 1897 in Sandersville, Georgia.

# CONTENTS

|    | Editor's Note                               | i  |
|----|---------------------------------------------|----|
| 1  | A Sign: The alteration of the day and night | 6  |
| 2  | 40 Years                                    | 11 |
| 3  | Fear God Alone                              | 15 |
| 4  | The Poison of Envy                          | 18 |
| 5  | Surah 29, "The Spider"                      | 23 |
| 6  | The Trial of the Nation                     | 26 |
| 7  | Why Are Messengers Raised?                  | 33 |
| 8  | A Stone of Stumbling                        | 39 |
| 9  | Jesus: God With Us                          | 46 |
| 10 | Out of Dust                                 | 57 |
| 11 | The Children of Israel                      | 61 |
| 12 | A Virgin People                             | 65 |
| 13 | Elijah Muhammad                             | 69 |
| 14 | The Death Plot                              | 75 |

A Saviour is Born

| | | |
|---|---|---|
| 15 | Elijah is Alive, in Power | 87 |
| 16 | The Resurrection of Faith | 91 |
| 17 | Warning to hypocrites and enemies | 97 |
| 18 | Muslim Fight Song | 100 |
| 19 | Rebirth of a Nation | 103 |
| | About the Final Call Foundation | 106 |
| | About the Editor | 108 |

## EDITOR'S NOTE

The edited transcript of this lecture is marked with
subheadings to facilitate the careful study of the words of
the Honorable Minister Louis Farrakhan.

In the Name of Allah, the Beneficent, the Merciful, The One God to Whom all praise is due, the Lord of the Worlds, Who came to us in the Person of Master Fard Muhammad, the long-awaited Saviour and Deliverer of the Black man and woman of America, and in the name of His true Servant and last Messenger, our beloved leader, teacher and guide, the Messenger of Allah, the Most Honorable Elijah Muhammad, I greet you my beloved Brothers and Sisters with the greeting words of peace in the Arabic language, *As-Salaam Alaikum*.

A Saviour is Born

I must say that you look so beautiful. I'm very filled up at this moment. I'm happy and thankful to Almighty God Allah for each and every one of you who came out today in the rain to say "welcome back" to the Nation of Islam. To those who came around me when I first stood up for the Honorable Elijah Muhammad, who felt that my life was in danger and that, if I were to stand for the Honorable Elijah Muhammad, I needed protection.

Those Brothers and Sisters who enveloped me in their care make it possible for us to be here today though we never can give the credit or take the credit from Almighty God Allah and His Messenger. I am grateful to Lu Palmer, Haki Madhubuti, Hannibal Afrik, Andy Thompson, and Vernon Jarrett. I'm grateful to Georgia Palmer, Rev. Al Sampson, Prince Asiel Ben Israel, Dr. Charles Knox, and Father George Clements. These men and women represent the total spectrum of Black thought, from Nationalists to

## A Saviour is Born

Christians, to Hebrew Israelites, Methodists, Catholics, even Socialists, Integrationists, and members of the Black Police—Howard Saffold and Renault Robinson of the Afro-American Police League.

How, then, can the Nation, in its rebirth, be an exclusive thing only for itself and its concerns? I'm here today because I was embraced by the totality of the Black community. So, we say to you that the Nation of Islam is not an exclusive order, but it is inclusive of every Black man, woman, and child in America and throughout the world.

Our mission is first to the Black people of America and then to Black people all over the world. I'm grateful to those Brothers and Sisters who helped me. I'm grateful to the National Laborers: Assistant Minister Herman, Supreme Captain Theron X, Assistant Supreme Captain Brother William J.X., and National Captain of the M.G.T. & G.C.C. Sister Christine Muhammad. To Minister Linward, Minister

## A Saviour is Born

Louis of the South, Minister Harold of the West, Minister Larry, all of you who sit to my right, my left, and in the audience who made it possible for us to come to this point in our development, words are just not adequate to say thank you. All I can do is pledge to you and, through you, to all Black America, my life. I am willing to spend my life for the freedom, justice, and equality of all Black people.

I have a special thanks to my wife, who has been with me in this work for 25 years and has been my wife for 27 going on 28 years, and a constant companion and constant comfort. I'm grateful to Allah (God) for my wife, Sister Farrakhan.

To my mother, who brought me onto this planet not knowing what her womb was carrying, I thank Allah (God) for my mother, for her laboring and suffering to give my brother and me the best that she could. Now, if it be the Will of Allah (God), I shall go on to do the work of the Honorable Elijah

## A Saviour is Born

Muhammad, that if history is kind to me for my labor, my mother's name will be remembered as long as my own, Sister Farrakhan.

Pardon me for taking this time to give thanks. The Honorable Elijah Muhammad told me, "Brother, you are going to reach the pinnacle of success in this world's life. But when you reach the top of the mountain, I hope you will remember who brought you there." So, I think it's proper that I take a moment and pay honor, respect, and thanks to those who brought me this far along the way.

Now, I pay a very special recognition to the Brother who came by my graveside when I had fallen backward, and whispered in my ear and helped me to see again. He's a very quiet Brother. He doesn't assume anything of himself. He likes to be in the background, but I think that Allah (God) would punish me if I didn't bear witness in public to what he did in private. That is Minister Bernard Cushmeer. He is around here somewhere taking pictures. Now, let us get into our work. Oh, wait a minute. I saw somebody I better not forget, a Sister who has been in the struggle for nearly 60 years. We call her the "Mother of the Struggle."

It wouldn't be proper if we didn't recognize Queen Mother Moore. And I hope he's here tonight—Brother Wali Siddiq, who met me in a restaurant and said, "Don't you think it's time?" All praise is due to Allah (God).

## A Sign: The alteration of the day and night

Brothers and Sisters, I'm going to say something to you today that some of you may think I'm a little touched. I have been among you as a follower of the Honorable Elijah Muhammad for 25 years. I'm sure most of you who have heard me either in person, on the radio, on television, or in private conversations, know me to be a very rational person, not given to insanity by any means. But I'm going to

## A Saviour is Born

say something and make an announcement today that probably will shock the known world. I'm going to say things today, by the Help and Power of Allah (God), that will shake the Christian world, the Muslim world, the Jewish world, the Communist world, and the political world. In fact, shake the world.

We didn't invite you here to waste your time. We invited you here to give you an earth-shaking announcement that, from this day forward, we will be challenged to prove. If you watch us and listen to us, I guarantee you every nation and every kingdom on earth will be rocked by the power coming from this tiny little budding nation that Jesus described as a mustard seed. When it germinates and grows and spreads its branches, every fowl and every bird will find refuge under its wing.

You are looking at the birth, not just of the Nation of Islam but the birth of the Kingdom of God Almighty on earth. You, Muslim scholars, are looking at the birth of the Kingdom of Islam. We called you here like the wise men of old who saw a star and traveled to where the baby was. The baby has no room to come to birth. She had to give birth in a manger or come to birth in a manger.

The wise men who saw the baby came bringing gold. What baby needs gold? All babies I know need milk, but here's a baby who needs gold. Gold for what? It's not talking about a child being born from a single mother. It's talking about a nation coming to birth that needs gold to build its institutions and carve out a destiny for itself.

In the Yusef Ali translation of the Holy Qur'an, in the 10th Chapter, 6th verse, it reads: *"Verily, in the alternation of the night and the day, and in all that Allah has created, in the heavens and the earth, are signs for those who fear Him."* There are signs for you in the alternation of the day and the night. We have a day to rise. We have a night to sleep. We see this alternation of day and night

## A Saviour is Born

in the development of all things. We have a time when we slumber and a time when we maximize our efforts in a conscious way. Nations have a time when they lapse into darkness, and they have a time when they spring forth again into new life.

In the history of the Honorable Elijah Muhammad among us, there was a rise, a fall, a rise again, and then another fall. In the alternation of the day and the night, there are signs for those who fear God. The Honorable Elijah Muhammad met a Man in Detroit, Michigan, a Man who gave many names, but the name He left us with was Master Fard Muhammad. Many people say that this somewhat "mystery" man, Master Fard Muhammad Who taught Elijah Muhammad, was some false man.

But, as you can tell a tree by the fruit it bears, you can tell a man by his works. Master Fard Muhammad met the Honorable Elijah Muhammad in 1931. The Honorable Elijah Muhammad immediately recognized him as the One Who the world was looking for when he heard the words coming out of His mouth, having read the Bible since he was a young boy. In the words coming out of this Man's mouth, he saw something corresponding to what he had been longing for and someone he had been hoping and longing for since he was a young boy. So, there was an instant love and an instant marriage between these two.

What Elijah Muhammad saw in Master Fard Muhammad, he was ordered not to go too far in teaching that Man's identity while He was among us, but that Elijah Muhammad should wait until after He was gone.

I must say the truth: The Honorable Elijah Muhammad said the same thing to me. When I was sneaking up on his identity and beginning to publish it over the radio, he called me one day and said, "Brother, don't go too far in that line, lest all the apples roll down out of the cart into the gutter."

## A Saviour is Born

I will tell you today what has been burning in my heart since the 60's when I first began to see the way I shall explain "sight" today.

**40 Years**

Master Fard Muhammad came to the Messenger, found him groping, showed him the way; found him an orphan, and took him in as the Qur'an teaches. He made him wise. The time of preparation for the Honorable Elijah Muhammad was between 40 and 41 months, nearly three and one-half years. He gave Elijah Muhammad, in that three and one-half years, enough wisdom to last for 40 years.

The Honorable Elijah Muhammad said to some of us that it would take him 40 years to understand his mission. **It would take him 40 years to understand his mission.**

Master Fard Muhammad suffered in the midst of us. He was well able to keep Himself from any

## A Saviour is Born

suffering. He was jailed among us. He was well able to keep himself from going to jail. He was struck in the mouth. He permitted Himself to be struck by one of the Lost-Founds.

When He told the Lost-Found, "I am your long-awaited Saviour and Deliverer," the man struck him. When the Messenger and some Brothers wanted to get on the man, He said, "Leave him alone. He'll be a good one, one of these days." What was it all for?

We are a people made blind, deaf, and dumb. The Mighty One came to lay down a path and make a demonstration for the Messenger. Seeing the path trodden by such a Holy One that all the Prophets predicted would come at the end of the world, seeing Him suffer to show His love for His Lost-Found nation, seeing Him go to jail, that Elijah Muhammad may learn the price of Truth in wicked America.

You cannot preach Truth in America. You cannot stand up for Truth in America and be afraid of

## A Saviour is Born

jail. You cannot stand up for Truth and the freedom of the people and be afraid of persecution or even death. All of this we must suffer to deliver an entire nation that yearns to be free.

What is the justification for His suffering? That the scriptures might be fulfilled. It says He came and made Himself obedient unto death and made Himself of no reputation. He didn't come telling you who He was. He came and did a work. When He was ready to go, I heard the Honorable Elijah Muhammad say that he looked out his window when his Beloved Master and Friend left and told him, "You don't need me anymore." He said, "Oh, yes, I do." And Master Fard Muhammad said, "Oh, no, you don't." He said he cried, and he cried, and he cried.

Two men met. They fell in love with each other. The first Man took the second man and impregnated him with a word. The second man became as a wife to the first Man, Who made him pregnant with truth and pregnant with a nation that had to be delivered from the clutches of White America. All praise is due to Allah (God).

In the three and one-half years or 40 to 41 months of the Honorable Elijah Muhammad's walking with Master Fard Muhammad, He laid out for His Servant a plan of action, which later became the Nation of Islam. The Honorable Elijah Muhammad said when he used to go to the prisons to retrieve or get Master Fard Muhammad, Master Fard Muhammad said to him: "As you, Elijah, came to My rescue at the beginning of your mission, at the end of it you will be in a condition that only I can get you out of."

I'm going to repeat that now. Brothers and Sisters, don't get tired. I want you to fasten your ears on my mouth and dissect the words. I'm going to say it again: **"As you came to My rescue at the beginning of your mission, at the end of it you will be in a condition that only I can get you out of."**

## A Saviour is Born

The Honorable Elijah Muhammad said it would take him 40 years to even understand his mission. So, "the end of it" meant the end of the first phase of his work, which was a preparatory phase because "40" or "4" represents preparation and foundation. The foundation for a government had to be laid. The preparation for the deliverance of a nation had to be made. At the end of that 40 years, the Messenger would be in such a terrible condition that only God Himself could get him out of it.

### Fear God Alone

The Honorable Elijah Muhammad always referred to Master Fard Muhammad as "The Saviour." When he looked at Master Fard Muhammad's picture, he would say, "The Saviour." He kept that word in front of us for 40 long years: The Saviour. Not without a reason, not without a purpose, not without an aim, he wanted to drive the point home. I have met with

## A Saviour is Born

not *a* saviour, *The* Saviour, that One that the world has been looking for.

A man stands up in America preaching what Elijah Muhammad preached in the midst of the most vicious enemy the world has ever known. This government and this Caucasian people are the murderers of God's prophets. They have murdered every Black leader who has stood up for justice for us. Whenever someone came with something they didn't like, they snuffed out his life. For Elijah Muhammad to be in America saying what he said, doing what he did, don't you know he had to have a Mighty Protector and a Mighty Saviour?

The Honorable Elijah Muhammad said, "If Allah (God), Master Fard Muhammad, cannot save me, it would show that He cannot save you." If Master Fard Muhammad, the God of Elijah, could not save His Messenger, then we are wasting time bearing witness to Master Fard Muhammad as the long-awaited Mahdi, long-awaited Saviour, and long-awaited Deliverer. We are wasting our time blowing our breath to proclaim Elijah Muhammad as that final One, the Seal of the Prophets and apostles of God.

In the Holy Qur'an, in the 5th Chapter, 67th verse: *"O Messenger, deliver that which has been revealed to thee from thy Lord; and if thou do it not, thou hast not delivered His message. And Allah will protect thee from men. Surely Allah guides not the disbelieving people."*

Here's a Messenger given a message to deliver, and the God of the Qur'an is comforting him, telling him, "Don't be afraid. Go and deliver My Message, and I will protect you from men." The Qur'an teaches the Messenger and, through him, you and me in these words: *"Me and Me alone should you fear. Pray to Me and I will answer you."* What is He saying to the Messenger? If you fear only Me, then you'll do My Will. But if you fear men as you ought to fear Allah (God), you will do the bidding of men.

Most of us have fears, Brothers and Sisters. Many of you are afraid to stand up for truth for fear that you might lose a job. You might lose some friendship. You might lose some promised reward. Most of us carry our fears with us daily. Many in this audience would have taken a stand for the Honorable Elijah Muhammad a long time ago but fear stopped us. Fear choked us. Here's a man given an assignment and told, "Me and Me alone should you fear."

I realize it's hot in here. I know that the auditorium theatre has many concerts in here where the place is jammed to the rafters, and people are in the aisles getting down. I'm sure they have air conditioning and can cool this off. Yes. But I know something's coming that no one will be able to cool off.

**The Poison of Envy**

Before Master Fard Muhammad took leave of His Messenger, the Honorable Elijah Muhammad, He gathered the Muslim community and told them to hear Elijah Muhammad. Then He left. The moment He got out of sight, they began to put up excuses as to why they shouldn't listen to the Honorable Elijah Muhammad. Hypocrisy arose out of the family of the Honorable Elijah Muhammad. His brother became jealous of him, who is the Messenger. What created envy and jealousy in the heart of his own brother?

Brother and Sister, you have it in the Bible and the Qur'an. After Adam was made, he had two sons, Cain and Abel. Two children, coming from the same loins of the same father, from the same mother, but one hates and seeks to murder the other because of envy in the brother's heart. What does that tell you?

Coming out of your mother's womb doesn't sanctify your relationship with one another. Coming out saying, "This is my brother. That's my mother. That's my daddy," doesn't make you a family because members of the same family can be sick with the

## A Saviour is Born

poison of envy. All praise is due to Allah (God). The brother of Elijah Muhammad was sick with the poison of envy.

In 1935, think of it—**1935**, he rose to displace his brother. For seven years—think of that—**seven years**, Elijah Muhammad ran in the wilderness until he exhausted the hypocrites. One of them said he would eat one grain of rice a day until Elijah Muhammad was dead. Why did they hate Elijah Muhammad?

Because he said that he was the Messenger of Allah (God) and began to tell the world Who Master Fard Muhammad was—that He was, in fact, the Living God Who had made His Appearance in the world as the prophets predicted. Now, they see honor coming to the Messenger. They see a little money coming to the Messenger. The hypocrites said, "Uh-huh, he's trying to take the money for himself." So, they decided to kill him. Think over that. Why are you going into this history, Brother Farrakhan? Because history is now repeating itself. If you know what was, you can better understand what is, and then you're ready for what is just around the corner. All praise is due to Allah (God).

After seven years of running, fleeing, and hiding, fulfilling that which is written of the Messenger, the government gets him by executive order of Franklin Delano Roosevelt. The President of the United States ordered Elijah Muhammad off the street.

They used the excuse that he was a draft dodger when, in fact, he was too old for the draft. The draft was from 18 to 44. Elijah Muhammad was then 45. Then, why did they take him off the street? What he was teaching of Islam would not allow young Black men who heard it to sacrifice their life for the infidels.

As long as Elijah Muhammad had the freedom to teach, White folks would not be able to use your Black bodies as tools of service to keep America free and White and to keep them in power to continue to oppress you and me. So, they had to get Elijah

Muhammad off the street. They put him in jail for five years. All along, people were trying to kill him.

We've heard him say the hypocrites saw him when he was in New York. One reached for the pistol in his pocket, but he couldn't get his hands out of his pockets. He stood there, his eyes staring out into space, and the Messenger said, "Allah (God) got you." He got in a cab and went immediately to Grand Central Station and got out of New York.

What was God doing with His Messenger? He was showing him, "Rely on Me. Trust in Me. I've got power over your enemy. Do My Will. Fear no man. As the Bible teaches you, to whom is the arm of the Lord revealed?" If a man rolls up his sleeve—not mine—and shows you his mighty arm, he's showing you his power. When God shows a man His Power, that man has no cloak anymore to fear the world and its temporary power.

## Surah 29, "The Spider"

When the government put him in jail, he did nearly five years from 1942. He got out in 1946. From 1946 to 1975 is 29 years. The 29th Chapter of the Qur'an is entitled, "The Spider." I would like to read a little of it so we can come to some agreement.

God introduces the chapter by saying, *Bismillah Irahman Irahim*—In the Name of Allah, the Beneficent, the Merciful. *Alif Laam Meem*, which the scholars say means, "I, Allah, am the Best Knower. *"Do men think that they will be left alone on saying, We believe, and will not be tried? And indeed We tried those before them, so Allah will certainly know those who are true and He will know the liars."*

At the end of 29 years, bringing him to 1975, making a total of 40 years that Elijah Muhammad worked independently of the Presence of Master Fard Muhammad—the Nation will go under a trial. The spider spins its web at the darkest hour of the night. You must be up early to catch a spider spinning.

## A Saviour is Born

Usually, when you wake up, the web is already spun. When the spider spins its web, all lightweight creatures that fall in the web get caught.

But scientists say if the fly can get out within three seconds, it can live. The spider can't see; it only feels. When the fly touches the web, it tries to get out. Sitting in the center of the web, the spider senses it and then moves quickly to the prey. If the prey gets out within three seconds, the spider has no meal. The interesting thing about the spider is that it injects something like a needle into the fly and injects enzymes that break down the fly's form. Then, the spider sucks the insides of the fly into himself, leaving the remains in the web.

What is God telling us in this chapter? God is telling us that, after 29 years of the effort of Elijah Muhammad to rebuild and after 40 years of a great, magnificent history, darkness will come over the Nation, and it will be a deep, deep darkness. In the dark

## A Saviour is Born

hour, a spider will come. You will have time to get out of the web, but it is a short time. You must make haste to get out because when that spider gets to you, he will fill you with enzymes and break down your form.

Look at all the Muslims who fell in the night. Their form has been broken down. Their moral form, spiritual form, and even physical form are no longer what they were because a spider injected them with a poisonous doctrine that broke down their form and he sucked them up.

Most of the Muslims who fell under that teaching actually lost themselves. Those who stay there, when a spider is able to suck them up, take on the form of the spider. If you listen to most of those who follow the Messenger's errant son, you find them mouthing his hatred for his father, mouthing his rebellion against his father. They have now taken on the form of the spider, and they only have a few moments more to get out from under it.

Because this day, we open this meeting up to all, no matter what your persuasion will be. But in a few days, we shall have nothing more to do whatsoever with any hypocrite. We will not. Though you be our mother, father, or family member, we will cut you off because now you are headed into the Chastisement of Allah (God). Some of us are going into blessings; others are going into cursing. Wait and see. Before the year is out, the Chastisement of Allah (God) will have descended on most of the hypocrites. It's beginning to drop on them now.

## The Trial of the Nation

What were the elements of this trial? Number one: It was announced to us that a man, in whom we all had hoped, had expired. That was a trial because he's the only man who ever meant anything of value to us. He meant more to us than mother, more than father, and more than friend. We knew that all men die, certainly. But none of us expected it at that time. With swift suddenness, a new leadership came up—a leadership that never worked to build the Nation and consistently opposed to the Messenger. But all of a sudden, this new leader came to the scene. We all bore witness to him and submitted, or the majority did.

The third element of the trial was the repudiation of the Messenger's position as the Messenger of God. Then, the God that Elijah Muhammad preached to us about for 40 years—in Whom we put our trust and confidence and Who brought us out of the most difficult period—was denounced and rejected.

The revelation that Allah (God) revealed to the Honorable Elijah Muhammad for our salvation is classified as a lie. The culture and the lifestyle coming up out of the wisdom of Muhammad were mocked and ridiculed. The Sisters took off their garments and threw them away. Some who love Muhammad stayed in their garment, no matter what happened. They held fast. If you, faithful followers of Messenger Muhammad, don't stumble over your Brother, you will have a mighty reward.

But if you stumble over me today, all of your faith through the dark hour will not get you the reward you've earned because now you're tinged with a hypocrisy that must be explained. The value of all the accomplishments of the Honorable Elijah Muhammad and the Muslims was cast aside.

Brothers and Sisters, the United States government was deeply involved in all of this. Listen carefully. The United States government was deeply involved. The Islamic world was deeply involved. Jewish, Christian, and Communist elements were also implicated. We can say then that there was a worldwide conspiracy to destroy, number one, Elijah Muhammad; number two, the Nation of Islam; and number three, the influence of them both. What was the purpose of destroying the Nation? What was the purpose of destroying the influence of Elijah Muhammad?

The purpose was to steal Black people on the part of the government. The government wanted to take you down to their doom, which has now arrived. The Arabs want to use you as a pawn in their political struggle. Jews want to manipulate the Black man for their purpose. White Christians want to keep up the deceit they have carried on for the last 500 years in the name of Jesus.

Communists realized that the Nation of Islam, when it's strong in the Black community, Communism can't get a root in there. So, they understood that if you destroy Nationalist ideas, Nationalist sentiment, Nationalist feeling, and religious feeling, the people have nowhere to go but to a Socialist or Communist idea. You all were part of the conspiracy. For a while, it appeared as though the plan was effective. However, look again.

## A Saviour is Born

Here we are. Obviously, the Power that has produced our second rise is greater than the power of the world that produced our fall. If the government doesn't want us here and works to destroy us; the Islamic world doesn't want us here and works to destroy us; the Communists work to destroy us; Jews and Christians work to destroy us—I'm not talking about Black Christians and Black Jews, I must make a distinction. If they worked to destroy us and, here we are, what does that tell you about the Power that brought us back into existence?

The world bears witness that we did die. You bear witness that the Nation died. Those of you who were in the workshops yesterday, and saw the Brothers and Sisters, bear witness that we are now alive again.

You also bear witness that no group that the United States ever destroyed came back to recapture its former glory, not one. As great as Marcus Garvey was, he never recaptured his former glory. As great as Noble

## A Saviour is Born

Drew Ali was, he never recaptured his former glory. But this is our first Saviours' Day in seven years in the city where they destroyed the Nation. This is the first.

To what Power can we attribute this phenomenon? Could the writers of scripture overlook this? Did the writers of scripture see this happening? And if they did, how did they write it? Where did they put it? How could we die right in your face and come back? You said to us, "Where y'all been? Where y'all been? Y'all look good."

Farrakhan died right in your face. You didn't hear from me for three years. All of a sudden, here you come, "Where you've been, Brother? We thought you were dead." I've got news for you. I was dead. If the writers of scripture didn't overlook it—and they didn't—then where is this in the scripture?

One day I was sitting with the Honorable Elijah Muhammad, and he pointed to his mouth and said, *"This mouth is not made to speak idle words. This mouth is made to speak the Will of God."* If this man's, Elijah Muhammad's, mouth was made to speak the Will of God, then nothing that he says from Allah (God) will fail, for the very integrity of God is wrapped up in God's Word.

Why is it so difficult for us and the world to believe that Allah (God) would intervene in our affairs and raise from the midst of Black people a messenger for our salvation? Every party is now coming up with an excuse to justify their denial of Elijah Muhammad's messengership. "He must be an imposter. He made it up. He forged it. We deem him to be a liar. Oh, he's of those deluded."

I want you to help me answer these questions. Brothers and Sisters, Christians, Muslims, Hebrew Israelites, Nationalists, Integrationists, Communists, Atheists, Agnostics—I think I covered everybody. Maybe I'll throw some colors in there, too—Black, Brown, Red, Yellow, and White. If you believe that

Allah sent prophets, messengers, and apostles to the people of the past, why do you refuse to acknowledge a man raised from among us today?

You believe that Moses came? You believe that Jesus came? You believe that Noah, Abraham, and Lot came? You believe that Prophet Muhammad (peace be upon him) of Arabia came? You do believe? Or **do** you? Ninety-nine percent of you are disbelievers in God. I'm going to say that again. **Ninety-nine percent of you are disbelievers in God**, and the other half of a percent are hypocrites. You don't believe in God. You are a liar because if you believe God did these wonderful things yesterday, what happened to Him? He can't do it today? No, you don't believe.

## Why are messengers raised?

I know what you're saying. You're saying, "But Jesus answered it all." The Muslims are saying, "Muhammad answered it all." Well, if they answered it all, what are we here for? If you tell me Christ is the answer—ad I bear you witness, he certainly is the answer—how come you haven't solved the problem? If Christ is the answer, and you've got the answer, and we've got the question, how come you haven't answered it? Because the Christ that you talk, you don't know. The Muhammad that you preach, you really don't understand. The God that you say you serve, you have no real confidence in Him.

Why are messengers raised? What is their function? What is their purpose? What are the conditions that justify the presence of a messenger? Are these conditions present among us and the world? If we are not to expect anyone else, why did all the prophets from all parts of the earth predict One coming after them? Why did God make a covenant or an agreement with the people of the earth through their prophets? There's not one people on the earth today that can get away from this critical question. If

## A Saviour is Born

Elijah Muhammad **is** the Messenger of Allah (God), you all are in trouble.

If he is not the Messenger of Allah, you don't have anything to worry about. You can continue in your foolishness. But if he **is** the Messenger of Allah (God), I'm telling you, Christian, you're in trouble. Jew, you're in trouble. Hebrew, you're in trouble. Agnostic, you're in trouble. If you deny this man God raised as a final warner before the end of America, you're going down with this beast. There is no more warning going to come to you.

Do you know why our little Black babies are being killed in Atlanta? They're being killed in Atlanta because Atlantans are dumb enough to believe that we've entered the millennium. You have a Black Mayor, a Black Chief of Police, Black County Commissioners, and a heavy Black bourgeoisie. Because they can eat in White folks' restaurants, go in White folks' stores, and sleep in White folks' hotels,

## A Saviour is Born

they swear that White folks have changed and are all right now. But now God is driving it home to you.

Every day a baby's gone. Not a grown man but a *baby* gone. You had your ribbons out for the hostages, but you don't have a ribbon out for your Black babies. You don't care about your Black babies. Brother and Sister, if we were alive, we'd march on Atlanta. If we were alive, we'd say, "Not again. You all either start finding the killer of our Black babies, or your White babies will start dying."

You think that's not fair? Do you think that this White man can go to the moon but can't find a murderer of our babies? Do you think this White man is able to spy on Black people and tell by the gas that they let out what they had for dinner but can't find the murderers of our babies? That's a d--- lie.

Your life is not worth a quarter in America. Your life is less than a dog's life in America. The White man will sit a dog at his table and not even ask you to

## A Saviour is Born

come in by the back door. He'll pick up a stray dog on the highway but leave you on the highway hungry, naked, and out of doors. He will stop your car if you run over a dog but will run over Black men, Black women, and Black children day and night, shoot you down like a beast in the street and then justify it by saying you attacked them. Don't you tell me we don't need a Saviour born for the Black man in America.

We need to be saved from our ignorance. Our ignorance is killing us, Brothers and Sisters. We need to be saved from our self-hatred. We need to be saved from our lust to destroy one another. We need to be saved from this brutal, self-defeating inferior psychology that White folks have put on us that makes it difficult for us to do anything of value without opposing and destroying one another.

We need a Saviour. I ask you, do Black people qualify for one? I appeal to God: Have we met the requirements?

## A Saviour is Born

If I meet the requirements to go to school and you deny me, why? If I meet the requirements to buy a home in a decent neighborhood and you deny me, why? If I meet the requirements to call down from heaven its blessings and mercy and a messenger and a warner and a Saviour and You, God, reject me, I ask You, why? Are You racist, too?

Do you know why you don't believe God raised a messenger for you? Do you know why it's so easy for you to deny the gift of God's Wisdom in a man from among yourselves? Because you have fallen so low in your estimation of yourself, you really don't believe God cares. Though you shout, though you sing, though you dance, though you run up and down the aisles, deep down inside you don't believe

God is interested in the affairs of Black folks. You don't believe. You don't believe Almighty God could do for you what He did for those before you. When a people think like that, when God does raise a messenger from the midst of that people, they always reject him.

Because they say, "Why would God speak to a n-----? Doesn't God have anything better to do? Oh, I can't believe that. What, a man from among us met with God?" They say, "No, that n-----'s lying. You know n------ lie. That n-----'s trying to rob you." Of what? You don't have anything. A man is trying to give you something. The Honorable Elijah Muhammad used to pay people in the city of Chicago to come and listen to him. He would give them a dollar if they sat in the temple for a few hours and heard what he had to say. He didn't come to rob you. He came to save you, Black man.

### A stone of stumbling

What is the reason that Arabs reject a messenger? I know how they cover it up. I'm talking to the Arabs in the audience. You cover it up by saying,

## A Saviour is Born

"Oh, no, it is written in the 33rd Surah, 40th verse, that Muhammad is not the father of any of your men, but he is the Messenger of Allah (God), the Seal of the Prophets. There is no messenger to come after Prophet Muhammad (peace be upon him)." I hear that coming out of an Arab's mouth, and then I watch the actions of the Arab world. Their actions are a denial of the confession of their faith. Hypocrites.

I want to expose the root of why you say that. If you sincerely believe that Prophet Muhammad of Arabia was the Seal of the Prophets, we could sit down together and reason and come to an equitable agreement. But no, Arab, deep down, you are a racist. You have never gotten past that nature of you, which is akin to the nature of the European devils. You, the Jew, and the other Europeans are all the same people. I'm not talking about the original Arab because he looks like somebody from 63rd and Cottage Grove. Arabs will deny you a messenger because, deep down inside, they have no respect for Blacks. They really don't believe that God could ever raise anything of value out of you.

Therefore, if you're going to be saved, it must come from Arabs. It can't come from you because n-- ---- ain't nothing. That's the underpinning of their hearts. They don't want to admit it. I'm sorry, this is open heart surgery today. To even reason with a Messenger coming up out of you represents, to Mecca and the Arab world, the loss of power and the scepter of rulership over the religion of Islam. They cannot, for the life of them, think that God would give the leadership to someone who looks like you.

One hadith, or saying, of Prophet Muhammad of Arabia (PBUH), is that he heard the footsteps of Bilal going into paradise before him. Bilal was a Black man, an Ethiopian. If the Prophet of Islam, a White man, heard the footsteps of Bilal going into paradise before him, and Bilal was an Ethiopian, a Black

African—what did Prophet Muhammad (PBUH) mean? Bilal was just a muezzin, the caller of the faithful to prayer. Why should he go into paradise before the Prophet? What was he trying to get the White Arabs to see and understand?

He knew something about the Black man and the future of Islam that you have yet to learn. Why are messengers raised? Brothers and Sisters, messengers are raised to explain, interpret, and teach because there are many things of scripture we don't understand. When God gives us a messenger, that messenger is sent to give understanding. Understanding brings unity among the people in the end. Messengers are raised to uplift fallen humanity.

Messengers are raised as warners and bearers of good news. Messengers are raised as examples of human conduct. Messengers are raised as inviters to Truth by Allah's (God's) Permission. Messengers are raised as a mercy to the people from the Beneficent

God. Do we qualify? Do we need somebody to explain things to us?

The Messenger used to say to us, *"I have to teach them everything."* He had to teach us how to go to toilet. Do you know that many of us do not actually know how to go to toilet? That's sad. The Messenger had to teach us the manners of civilized people. We don't know yet how to act in such way that the world will respect and accept us. The Messenger had the hardest job of any man who ever lived. He worked with the worst of the people, but he was successful.

If messengers are to uplift fallen humanity, are we downtrodden and in need of uplifting? Are messengers bearers of good news? Don't we need somebody to tell us some good news, Brother? Don't we need examples of righteous conduct in front of us?

Some of you say he was not an example of righteous conduct. I beg your pardon. He was the most perfect example of righteous conduct, but you have made a grave mistake in judging what you don't understand.

The Bible teaches that God is going to lay in Zion a stone, a tried stone, a precious cornerstone, but it's a stone of stumbling. Many of you have stumbled over the domestic life of the Honorable Elijah Muhammad. Brothers and Sisters, messengers are raised to bring life mentally, morally, spiritually, socially, and economically to a people who are dead. We certainly stand in need of a life-giving force.

Historians say that at the time of the birth of Muhammad (PBUH), civilizations stood teetering on the brink of disaster. How much more so now is civilization teetering on the brink of disaster? We are living at a time that Muhammad (PBUH) envisioned that he was a sign of and that the world during his time was a sign of. Look at the world now. America has the power to kill the earth 30 times over. Russia has the same power. The whole world faces annihilation,

## A Saviour is Born

devastation, and total destruction. If before Muhammad (PBUH) was born, the world stood that way, and it ushered in his birth, whose birth does the condition of the world call for now?

This condition does not call for a mere prophet. No. In fact, when you call yourself a prophet, you're really putting yourself out of it because this is not the day of prophets. There's nothing to prophesy. The prophets have already prophesied it. If you're a prophet, what do you have to prophesy? Now, your mouth is shut up. What is called for today is not a prophet. What is called for today is one greater than a prophet. The condition calls for the birth of a mighty Saviour. The condition calls for the Coming of God Himself, for only God and His Power can save you, Brother and Sister, from the fall of America.

Only God can save the Hebrew Israelites in the jaws of the beast in Israel. Only God can save Mother Africa from neo-colonialism.

## A Saviour is Born

This is a scriptural subject. Sometimes you like to hear me get on White folks. But, Brother and Sister, we must get on you because if we don't get on you, White folks are not going to get on you; they're going to kill you. By 1990, most of you in this audience will be dead. That's how serious it is.

Some of you are so hip that you don't even want to look at the Bible. Others are so hip the Qur'an looks like a book of fairytales. But these two books are the most powerful books in the hand of man. If they're understood, it is a plan for your salvation.

### Jesus: God with us

Moses, the first major prophet, didn't leave anything to be desired. Moses knew somebody greater than him was coming. In Deuteronomy, the 18th Chapter, 18th verse, God is talking to Moses: *"I will raise them up a prophet from among their brethren, like unto thee, and will put my words in his mouth; and he shall speak unto them all that I shall command him."* Moses didn't believe that it was him. Moses knew better. When Moses prayed for a vision of that last one, the scripture says Moses fell down in a swoon.

Bear with me now. This is very crucial. Jesus also admitted one greater than him was coming. In the Book of John, 14th Chapter, 16th verse. Jesus says: *"And I will pray the Father, and he shall give you another Comforter, that he may abide with you forever."* Jesus is not telling the people, "I'm going to be with you forever." Jesus says, "I'm going to pray to the Father that He'll give you another Comforter. "Another Comforter" means somebody else. Jesus is talking in the first person, about somebody else in the third person: and *he* will abide with you forever.

Prophet Muhammad (PBUH) is made to repeat the prayer of Abraham and Ishmael. God puts it in his mouth and makes Muhammad say it to the people: *"When Abraham and Ishmael raised the foundation of the House: Our Lord! accept from us; Surely Thou art the Hearing, the Knowing."* (Surah 2:127) Listen to the prayer: *"Our Lord! and make us both submissive to Thee and (raise) from our offspring a nation submissive to Thee, and show us our ways of devotion and turn to us (mercifully), surely Thou art the Oft-returning (to mercy), the Merciful."* (Surah 2:128).

Notice the attributes used here. God is the Hearing, the Knowing. He's the Oft-returning to Mercy. He is the Merciful. It says, "Our Lord, and raise up in **them** a Messenger." He's already the Messenger. He's present. He didn't say "and raise up in *us*," meaning the Arabs. "Raise up in them."

Who is "them"—raise up in them a Messenger who shall recite to them Thy messages and teach them the Book and the Wisdom. The book is the Bible. The wisdom is the Qur'an. Prophet Muhammad (PBUH) is giving the people the Qur'an. So, this man couldn't teach the Qur'an if the Qur'an wasn't in existence. This is a man coming *after* Muhammad of Arabia (PBUH).

## A Saviour is Born

Look at the attributes that God uses here. "Surely thou art the Mighty, the Wise." You have Hearing, Knowing, Oft-returning to Mercy, the Mighty, the Wise. What did Prophet Muhammad (PBUH) say in his hadith? He said that *"the world will not pass away until a man of my house rules over the Arabs."*

He's telling the people that a ruler coming out of his house will rule the Arabs. His name will be similar to my name. His name is Muhammad. The Qur'an prophesied one coming under the name *Ahmad*, which is another way of saying Muhammad: His father's name will be similar to my father's name. *"He will fill the earth with justice and equity as it has been filled up with tyranny and oppression."* (Hadith)

Muhammad of Arabia (PBUH) filled the earth with the Qur'an, but he didn't fill it with justice. He did not stop tyranny and oppression. So, what does this mean? This means that the work of Prophet Muhammad (PBUH) would be overshadowed by

## A Saviour is Born

wickedness, tyranny, and oppression among the Arabs and the whole world. This One who comes will fill the earth with justice. He must be greater than Muhammad because Muhammad is saying that he will fill the earth with justice. Muhammad couldn't do that. All the prophets prophesied a superior one coming. Now, we're at the most crucial part of this lecture.

He is known under various names. The Jews are looking for the Messiah. The Christians are combing the horizon the Christ. The Muslims are looking for the Mahdi. The Jews say it's time now that the Messiah should appear. The Jews don't recognize Jesus of 2,000 years ago as that one. The Christians say the time is nigh that Christ should reappear. And the entire Muslim world is nervously expecting the sudden appearance of the Mahdi. Are we looking for three different men? Or are we looking for one man described and characterized by different branches of belief under three different names? Do you have on your diving suits because we have to go down in the water. We're going to come up, but we've got to get deep now.

I'm going to shock a few Muslims and make a few Christians happy. The greatest truth to come to the world is hidden in the truth of the man under the name "Jesus." I'm going to say it again. **The greatest truth to come to the world is hidden in the truth of the man under the name "Jesus."** There are two powerful aspects of that truth.

Number one is the relationship of Jesus to God. Jesus breaks down the veil between man and God. I'll say it again. **Jesus breaks down the veil between man and God.** Jesus makes man understand the divinity in his human nature. That's the number one aspect. The number two aspect: Did Jesus escape from death? These two powerful aspects of the man Jesus have the whole religious world rocking and reeling because the scholars are trying to find the difference between the historical Jesus and the prophetic Jesus.

The Muslims say, yes, Jesus is coming back, but they're all confused about whether he died on the cross, was he killed, this, that, and the other? All praise is due to Allah (God). Scholars, you might as well put your books down. Put them down and come listen to the babes. The scripture says, "I thank thee, Father in heaven, for keeping these things from the wise and the prudent man, and revealing them unto babes." (Matthew 11:25).

No wise men know this. No prudent men know this. God has revealed the utmost truth of these scriptures that confound the scholars of the world to the babes. Little, old, Black people in America that you call n------. Brothers and Sisters, a Saviour is born.

In the Book of Matthew (1:21), it reads: "And she shall bring forth a son, and thou shall call his name Jesus: for he shall save his people from their sins."

## A Saviour is Born

Isaiah, 7th Chapter, 14th verse, tells us the same thing but uses a different word. Isaiah says, "Behold, a young woman shall conceive, and bear a son and shall call his name Emmanuel." How did Emmanuel become Jesus? How did the young woman become the virgin?

All the virgins in the audience—I have to pause on that one. That's a crime that you can say that and know that you're hardly looking at any. That shows we're a people morally destroyed. Your common sense tells you virgins don't have babies. Any one of you who has had a baby, were you a virgin when you had it?

I know what you're saying. "It was a miraculous thing." I guess so. If it happened back then, can it happen again today? Let your baby come home to you, pregnant and tell you she was going by the school one day, and the Holy Ghost rushed out of the school and touched her. She says, what I have here is of the Holy Ghost. Since you believe it already happened, why couldn't it happen to your daughter?

## A Saviour is Born

But you'd whip that girl until she brought that baby here. You would tell her, find me the "whatever you call him" because you know if there isn't a man, there isn't a child. How did the virgin conceive? You must know today because a Saviour is born.

Matthew, 1st Chapter, 23rd verse reads: "Behold, a virgin shall be with child, and bring forth a son, and thou shall call his name Emmanuel, which being interpreted is, God with us." Now, we have a key. Let's see what it will open.

Here's a child being born and a young woman, Isaiah calls her. Matthew calls her a virgin. We can get some juice out of both terms. A woman will conceive the child, and the child will be called Emmanuel. Matthew says, "Thou shall call his name Jesus."

The interpretation of "Emmanuel" is "God is with us." So, when Jesus came into the world, God stepped in among men. Think about it. His work among the people was God working in a man. His miracles among the people were God interacting with the people, through Jesus.

They looked at Jesus and were looking at God, but they didn't know who they were looking at. They heard his voice, but they didn't know who they were listening to. They lied on him. They cheated him. They scorned him. They mocked him. They ridiculed him. They plotted against him. They didn't know they were plotting against the agent of God, the emissary of God, the true witness of God. The divinity of his nature became one with the divine nature of God. They crucified him.

After three days, they said he rose from the dead. He said he had to go through this to be ready for a power coming to him. He had to be deserving of a crown that would be given to him. Everything under the heavens, except God Himself, would be placed in his hands. He would be powerful over all things to show that man has the power to become like God and the master of the universe. Jesus showed man our true nature after man had fallen under the arch-deceiving devil and was living like a dog. Jesus came to show men you can reverse this and be a perfect reflection of the Divine Being. So now, we must search for this Jesus.

We must find this Jesus. When we find him, we must hold on to him, for if we hold on to him, we're holding on to God. If we hold on to him and his Father, we will be called the Children of Light, and there will be no darkness in us.

Isaiah, the prophet, looked and saw him coming. Isaiah wrote (9:6-7), "For unto us a Child is born, and unto us a Son is given; and the government shall be upon His shoulder. And His name shall be called Wonderful, Counselor, The Mighty God, The Everlasting Father, The Prince of Peace. Of the increase of His government and peace there shall be no end." The Jesus of 2,000 years ago said, "I'm going to pray to the Father, He will send you another

Comforter, and he will abide with you forever." Who is that "he" that Jesus saw? That Isaiah saw? That was the Everlasting Father Who came bringing a government.

## Out of dust

This Jesus, his likeness with Allah (God) is as the likeness of Adam. Adam was an Original man, an original type created from dust. Christ is an Original man. What do you mean "Original?" Christ is the first man of a new order.

Where is that souvenir journal? This book, we kept trying to get it together. We finally ended up with 76 pages. The Honorable Elijah Muhammad taught us that the diameter of sunlight, the diameter of the universe is 76 quintillion miles. He said it was 76 trillion years ago that God created the sun.

The 76th Surah of the Qur'an is called *Al-Insan*, "The Man." From the time God created Himself in darkness and created the universe, the universe has been groaning under the burden of its search for perfection. As the diameter of sunlight is 76 quintillion miles, and the sun was created 76 trillion years ago, at the end of 76 trillion years, the search of the Original God for the perfection of man would come into existence. The only reason history rises and falls is because there's an imperfection in the nature of man.

You cannot change history until you change the nature of man. Jesus comes into the world and is put through trial and tribulation, ups and downs. God takes him up and hurls him down. God wants to beat him into a shape where a perfect man would evolve out of darkness again. Out of the nature of that perfect man, he would be an original type. All those who flowed to him would bask in his perfection.

Scripture says we know not how we shall look but know that we shall be changed in the twinkling of an eye, and we shall be like Him. If he, the Original

## A Saviour is Born

man, perfect, made from dust as the Original man called Adam, then we who have been reduced to nothing—dust—have hope.

If God made the first man from nothing, and in the 76th Chapter entitled, "The Man," it reads that once upon a time, man was nothing that we should speak of. At one time, the White man was nothing that we should speak of. His history in the caves of Europe, he was nothing. Look at how he has grown. You are nothing now. You've been reduced to dust. Do you think that you won't be raised out of that state? As God made the first man, Adam, from nothing, he makes Christ from nothing.

Gird up now. The Holy Qur'an is scripture, but it is also historic. If you can't appreciate the weight of this, maybe one day, when you have evolved, you will understand this lecture today better than you understand it now. *[This is of the tidings of the things unseen which We reveal to thee. And thou wast not with them when they cast their pens (to decide) which of them should have Mary in his charge, and thou wast not with them when they contended one with another.]*—the 44th verse of the 3rd Chapter—and that number 44 is very significant. The next verse (45) reads: *"When the angels said: O Mary, surely Allah gives thee good news with a word from Him (of one) whose name is the Messiah, Jesus, son of Mary, worthy of regard in this world and the Hereafter, and of those who are drawn nigh (to Allah), and He will speak to the people when in the cradle and when of old age, and (he will be) one of the good ones."*

Jesus didn't speak to the people in the cradle. He was a very young man when he started teaching but he died at 36. Scripture says 33. So, he never did speak when he got old. The historical Jesus never grew old.

Who is this Messiah, this Jesus, this son of Mary who will speak in the cradle and speak when of old age? Mary said: *"My Lord, how can I have a son and man has not yet touched me? He said, even so, Allah creates what He pleases, and when He decrees a manner, He only says to it, Be, and it is."* Showing you that the same active Will of God involved in the first creation is involved in the birth of the Messiah.

*"And Allah will teach him the Book and the Wisdom, the Torah and the Gospel."* That can't be Muhammad (PBUH). That must be a man who comes after the wisdom of the Qur'an is here, after the Book is here, after the Torah is here, after the Gospel is here—but God is going to teach this man the uttermost depth of the meaning of all those books.

## The Children of Israel

It says, "Make him a Messenger to the Children of Israel." Who are the Children of Israel? If you have a dollar in your pocket, take it out and look at it. Be careful. Hold it tight. Look on the back of it. They say money talks. We just never knew what it said. In the right-hand corner, you see an eagle with nine feathers in its tail, arrows, an olive branch, six white stripes, and

## A Saviour is Born

seven red stripes. All of this is heavy. The 13 stars over the eagle's head represent the Seal of the President of the United States and the government of America.

If you took a pen, starting from that top star, and came down the line, went across and over, you'll find two inverted triangles, creating the Star of David. We're talking about the Children of Israel. This Israel that we're talking about is the Israel that wrestled with God. His name was Jacob or *Yacub*. After he prevailed, his name was changed to Israel. This is not talking about Black Israel. This is not talking about original Israel. This is talking about the prevailing power in the world under the name of Israel.

Brother and Sister, America also is Israel. That's why she and those Jews are locked up together because they're on in the same—only this one hides and that one manifests. How could the Jews only be six million and run everything? How could he master all of the T.V. communications and hide behind White

## A Saviour is Born

Anglo-Saxons? How could he master the educational system? How could he master the monetary system? This is Israel, the rebel against God.

Who are the Children of Israel? Look up, children. You're just like your no-good, rebellious foster father. The White man is a rebel against God, and that's what he made you. You are a rebellious, hard-hearted, stiff-necked, and vile people. That's not your nature, but that's the way you've been reared by White people. Tell me I'm lying. Look at your condition, Brother. You're not submissive to God. You're a rebel against God. If God tells you the way He wants it, you want to change His way to suit your rebellious idea.

You try to change the church over. You call it Jesus' church, but it's not his. It's a rebellious people in the church. Do you think if Jesus came back today, he would accept half of you who call yourselves Christians? He'd kill you.

## A Saviour is Born

Jesus doesn't have gays in his church. Jesus doesn't have any lesbians. Jesus doesn't want any liars. Jesus doesn't want you even if you're effeminate acting, according to the Book. Jesus doesn't want any fornicators and adulterers. How will you make it, Christians, with your rebellious self? Turn the church of God into a house of abominations, but you use Jesus' name to shield your dirty religion. No good. No, Christian. You're condemned.

He said, "Make him a messenger unto the Children of Israel (saying): I have come to you with a sign from your Lord"—what is the sign that you are coming with? *"I determine for you out of dust the form of a bird, then I breathe into it and it becomes a bird with Allah's permission, and I heal the blind and the leperous, and bring the dead to life with Allah's permission; and I inform you of what you should eat and what you should store in your houses. Surely there is a sign in this for you, if you are believers."*

## A virgin people

Now, let's find Jesus. Is this Black History Month? Why did they give you a month? Isn't it true that they gave you a month to study your history, and every day of the year, you're reading their history? How can you be justified in studying your history for one month when time doesn't even show when you began on the planet? How can you be justified in reading White folks' history, which is a moment in time, and leaving your own history unread? What you study this week is not really your history. You're just studying the accomplishments of a slave who made it under the oppression of his master while he still wears the name of his master. So, he's not yet making any history. This is his accomplishments in the history of White people. Do you agree?

During this month, when you're trying to research something valuable in yourself, suppose I told you that the greatest value that the whole world has

## A Saviour is Born

been looking for and seeking is coming out of you. Scripture says, *"Can any good come out of Nazareth?"* They said Jesus was of Nazareth. Can any good come out of 30 million Black people in America? Let's look and see.

The Jesus of the New Testament does his work on the Sabbath day. If a day with the Lord is as a thousand years, then to do his work on the seventh day is to do his work in the seven thousandth year from the making and fall of Adam. From Adam to Moses is 2,000 years. From Moses to Jesus is 4,000 years. So, when Jesus worked 2,000 years ago, he was working not on the Sabbath day but on the fifth day. That's why Paul saw Jesus as a man born out of due season.

But now we are in the 7,000th year from the making of the White race. So, you should look for that one who heals, gives sight to the blind, gives hearing to the deaf, gives speech to the dumb, raises the dead to life, and cleanses the leper and the palsy. Look for him on the Sabbath day. You're living in the seventh day,

## A Saviour is Born

the 7,000th year from the making of the Caucasian people. Where is Jesus?

Where shall we look for him? Is he going to come out of the East? Shall he be found in China? Let's go to the isles of the Pacific, maybe he's there. Scripture says, "I call my son out of Egypt." If he's coming out of Egypt, what Egypt? Egypt now? Don't look there. That Egypt needs to be destroyed and is about to be.

Shall we look for him coming out of Israel. No. Israel is about to be wiped from the face of the earth. That state that you call Israel, is going. Take it or let it alone. God intends to kill everything in that area, just about, and brighten it up for the return of the people for whom the Holy Land rightly belongs. No Arab, you're not going to inhabit the holy places. Neither you, Jews. Your days of inhabiting the holy places is over. God is going to remove you. Where shall we look for Jesus?

## A Saviour is Born

A virgin shall conceive—there's the clue. A virgin is coming up. The term virgin, when it's talking about a woman, means one who has never been touched by a man. Sister, if you've never been touched by a man, then you haven't been introduced to the germ of life that creates and fashions new life. So, a virgin is going to conceive. Who's the virgin? It's a people who have never had intercourse with God.

You have never had a relationship with God. "Don't tell me I don't know God." Stop. If you say God is Beneficent, God is merciful, God is all wise, God is powerful, then we should see some of these attributes manifesting in you if you had a relationship with Him. You don't have any love for yourself, yet you say God is love. Where is that love in you? God is power. Where is that power in you? God is wisdom. Where's the wisdom in you? You're a virgin.

White folks, like a man who has a virgin daughter and she's sharp and ready, he watches the door. He doesn't let her answer when a knock comes, he goes to the door. "She's not having any company today. Move out. I know what you're looking for, you're looking for trouble, boy." That's the way White folks have been by you. Ever one of your people that would come to you, they block them. "Don't go up to them, n------. They're crazy. They're savage. Don't infect them with African thought, African culture. Stay away from them. They don't like you."

He's like a father who wants to protect the virginity of his daughter. White people call you "my negro." He doesn't like anybody teaching his negro anything other than what he put in you. You have never known a man. Any time a man got close to you to bring about new life, they aborted it.

## Elijah Muhammad

The Bible says he comes without observation as a thief in the night. The Bible says he comes in sinful flesh to condemn sin in the flesh. When Master Fard Muhammad came to North America, He looked like the Caucasian—fulfilling the scripture. He was made in such way that he could slip in unnoticed. He got in like a thief in the night.

His object was to make one of you pregnant with new life. He met with a man named Elijah under the cover of darkness and taught him for three and one-half years. That's the time given to Jesus' ministry. Then, he went away. There is a 40-day ministry of Jesus also. Master Fard Muhammad goes, and a little man named Elijah is born.

We see him darkly and dimly. For many years we called him, Mr. Muhammad, Elijah Mahmoud. Later, during the time of Malcolm X, we started calling him the Honorable Elijah Muhammad, Messenger Muhammad. He's growing among us.

He's doing things that we see and it's amazing, but we haven't caught on yet. He takes junkies and he

## A Saviour is Born

straightens them up. You bear witness to this. We came to the Messenger bent over. When he got finished with us, we were walking tall. We came to him with our skin dark. When he got finished talking to us, we began to shine, eyes bright.

Sisters came to him with the mini-dress and when they looked around, sister had on an ankle-length dress, felt too dignified to put on that filth anymore. The Nation of Islam was born out of those who were the worst of the people: the wine head, the hustler, the convict, the prostitute. It was only in the late 40's, in the middle 50's that somebody with some college education came to the Nation. This is the way all the prophets began.

As Muhammad began to grow, in 1959 at the Uline Arena in Washington, D.C. where they jailed the Honorable Elijah Muhammad, he comes back to Washington with an army. The brothers looked like they were uniforms—dark suits, red ties, shiny ball

## A Saviour is Born

heads. The police shaking, "Here comes the Muslims." The FBI escorted the Messenger down Pennsylvania Ave like he was a head of state. Parked outside of the house where he was, in the rain on their motorcycles and wouldn't move. Some of us were there. In the Arena, he talked to the government of America like America was his child.

It wasn't six months later that *Time* magazine, *Newsweek* magazine, and other magazines began to write about Elijah Muhammad. But now they're frightened of him so they call him an ex-convict. They said he went to prison. His national spokesman, Malcolm X at that time, they said he was a convict. "They're nothing but a bunch of thugs." They got Thurgood Marshall to speak against us. They got Ralph Bunche to speak against us. They got the NAACP to speak against us. They got Martin Luther King, Jr. to speak against us. Because Elijah now was preaching separation and the doom of America.

## A Saviour is Born

Meanwhile, back at the ranch in Washington, J. Edgar Hoover, watching the movement of Black people, was looking for a messiah. What did J. Edgar Hoover know that you didn't know? What did J. Edgar Hoover know about you and what you should expect? Some of these dumb Negro leaders talking about, "We keep looking for a Messiah but a Messiah is not what we need." Shut up, chump. That's exactly what you need. That's exactly what the scriptures prophesied would come to you. Not just a man but *the* man. The man for all time, the Messiah, Jesus the son of Mary. What would he do?

He would determine from dust the form of bird. How would you take dust and make a bird, breathe into it and it became a bird. Birds represent men who are able to soar into the lofty regions of wisdom and power. Here is a man determining a bird out of dust—you, dust. Elijah Muhammad said I will make a bird out of this. What do you mean you're going to make a bird? I'm going to make something to float and fly above the kingdoms of the world. I will take dust, fashion it, breathe into it, and it will be a bird by Allah's (God's) Permission.

Did you see Malcolm flying? Did you see Malcolm **flying?** You didn't look down when you saw Malcolm. You looked up. But who made that bird? Who formed him out of dust. Who breathed into his nostrils? You say, "Oh no, he was self-taught." Alright, well if he didn't do it once, he couldn't do it twice. But if he did it once, then he could do it again and again and again and again, and then some more.

Cassius Clay. He comes up, just an ordinary fighter, a dumb fighter. It's the truth. The Honorable Elijah Muhammad said, "I'm going to make a bird." He fashioned him out of dust. Dust means you're doing nothing, you become nothing, you're reduced to a particle that has no weight in society at all. You're just nothing. The Honorable Elijah Muhammad breathed

## A Saviour is Born

into him. Next thing, you looked up. You didn't look down. You looked up, and there was Ali. How pretty he was, floating like a butterfly, stinging like a bee. Floating high above. As long as he remembered his teacher, he was flying high.

Now, you have two fallen stars. Malcolm turned on his teacher and his wings were clipped. You saw a bird going right down. Look at Muhammad Ali. You see a man turned on his teacher and you see a bird coming down.

### The death plot

The Honorable Elijah Muhammad had a nation coming up like that. When Adam Clayton Powell was gone, they knew Martin Luther King, Jr. was not the Messiah. The devil isn't a fool. He can weigh you up just that quick. As the Bible teaches you, the devil knew Jesus before the disciples knew him. And they knew the Time.

## A Saviour is Born

These aren't dumb White folks. White folks listened to Martin Luther King, Jr., summed him up, and said, "He's mine because he doesn't want to leave me. He doesn't want to see me go. He wants to be my brother, not my brother-in-law, so he's a fool." He doesn't understand he can't be the Messiah.

They said Stokely (Carmichael) was the Messiah. Stop it. He's just a young man coming out of college. He hardly knows himself. He had promise but promise is not the real thing. They looked at Malcolm. They knew Malcolm was powerful as long as he was tied to that source. Many of you think Malcolm could make it on his own, but I'm telling you, Brother and Sister, the fatal mistake that Malcolm made was to cut himself from the Honorable Elijah Muhammad.

Some of you say, "Malcolm grew and he outgrew Elijah." How could he outgrow Elijah Muhammad and the Teaching of Elijah Muhammad is more in vogue now than it was when he was present

## A Saviour is Born

among us. How are you going to outgrow that man? H--- no! Most of you who think you have outgrown him, haven't even come up to his shoe top yet. You're just a rebellious people.

They got rid of Malcolm after they separated Malcolm from the Messenger. They got him. They got rid of Martin Luther King, Jr. They murdered him. How many of you believe the United States government had something to do with the murder of Martin Luther King? I'll raise my hand too. How many of you believe that the United States government had something to do with the murder of Malcolm X?

How many of you believe and know that the United States government was responsible for breaking the movement of the UNIA and deporting the Honorable Marcus Garvey? How many of you know and believe that the government was responsible for the death, under very suspicious terms, of Noble Drew Ali?

## A Saviour is Born

What is this telling you, Brother? There hasn't been any Black man standing up like this that the government wasn't plotting on. The government was plotting Elijah Muhammad's death. They said, "He's old. We'll wait on him to die." I have something to tell you now. We're at the end now. As the messenger began to get more and more powerful, the ranks of the Messenger began to fill up with unsavory characters. Around the Messenger was a ring of hypocrites. We didn't know it. They all looked good.

The Qur'an says Jesus started to open up to his disciples to tell them more about who he was. That's when he perceived disbelief on their part. According to the Qur'an, Jesus perceived disbelief in them. So, he asked the question, "Who are my helpers in Allah's Way." And the disciples answered, we are Allah's. Then it says, "and the Jews planned and Allah also planned and Allah is the Best of planners." What did the Jews plan and who are the Jews?

## A Saviour is Born

First, the United States government was planning Elijah Muhammad's death. We have information from the Freedom of Information Act of the counterintelligence program of the United States government that Elijah Muhammad was marked for "extermination" or "elimination."

They could not kill Elijah Muhammad as they would kill a man like Martin Luther King because we, the followers of Elijah Muhammad, were the most disciplined, organized group of Black people anywhere to be found. What White folks said was not that they are violent, but they have a potential for it, that if they ever unleash it, they would be the fuse that sets off the dynamite. If they were going to kill Elijah Muhammad, it had to be done in a way where it wouldn't spark revolution. The plan had to involve the inside as well as the outside.

It was on several levels. The government had a plan. The Arabs had a plan. The hypocrites had a plan.

## A Saviour is Born

And the Messenger's family had a plan. They are his family, they're just not too good. Allah (God) and His Messenger are judging them. I have to tell the truth. I don't give a d--- who it hurts.

The government had an overall plan to destroy us completely. The Arabs tested the Messenger. They offered the Messenger $20 million if the Messenger would send some of his students in the University of Islam to study in Medina, Riyadh, and Mecca.

The Messenger told the Arabs to go to hell. He got so loud at the dinner table that they heard him almost on the third floor, telling those devils, that he would not waste the life of one of you going to Mecca to learn about some spook mystery God for $20 million. He told them that "Allah (God) is sufficient for me."

The man who confessed to me is Dr. Ezzeddin Ibrahim, a very highly placed Arab in the United Arab Emirates and a leader in the Rabitat or the World

## A Saviour is Born

Muslim League. He confessed to me that they said that since they couldn't change the old man, they started working on members of his family and his laboring staff, trying to teach them prayers the way of Orthodox Islam, trying to bring them into what they call the "true religion." How little you really understand the Book you say you believe in.

The Arab way of devotion is not our way. God has given us a different way of devotion today, just like he gave Muhammad a different qibla or a different focal point for himself to look upon. *"And the people asked, 'why did they change their Qibla?'"* This is for Muslims—we can pray the way you pray, or we don't have to, and you can't condemn us as being non-Muslims by your misunderstanding of the Qur'an.

What the Caucasians and White Arabs need as the sunnah of the prophet (PBUH), the Black man does not need because by nature he's what they're trying to become. The Arabs are planning.

## A Saviour is Born

The government is planning. The hypocrites among our followers are also planning. Some members of the Messenger's family are beginning to say, "He is ill. He cannot go on. We'll take it over. We'll take it over." The conspiracy is on four different levels. Allah (God) says in the Qur'an, "and the Jews planned and Allah also planned and Allah is the best of planners."

The Messenger is in Mexico. He takes sick. They fly him from Mexico, past hospitals in Mexico City which have some of the best doctors in that particular thing that they said the Messenger had, to Mercy Hospital, a Catholic hospital in Chicago.

He lays in the hospital, and he is getting well. Many who visited him there are in this audience today and can bear witness that the Messenger was recovering. Every time, the Messenger got sick, the ears of the devils and hypocrites went up like a rabbit's, hoping for his death. Many in this audience who were close to the Messenger knows this of him—that man

## A Saviour is Born

would be brought right to death's door; he would be almost in a coma state in the morning and that evening he'd be at the dinner table, teaching as though nothing was wrong with him.

Why do you think Allah (God) would bring the man right to death and snatch him back, bring him right to death and snatch him back, bring him right to death and snatch him back. What was Allah (God), the Saviour saying to His Messenger? What was He trying to get him to see and understand?

When the Messenger was in that hospital, he told a visitor, "I expect to be coming out tomorrow." That night, they said his condition took a turn for the worse. In the 2nd Surah of the Holy Qur'an, 72nd verse, it read: *"And when you (almost) killed a man, then you disagreed about it. And Allah was to bring forth that which you were going to hide."*

The scholars universally agree that this is referring to Jesus, but they don't know how it fits. They

## A Saviour is Born

had planned to kill him and then they disagreed about it afterwards. Then Allah (God) was going to bring forth what they were going to hide. What is it that they have been hiding for six years?

That Elijah Muhammad didn't lay down in Mercy Hospital and die of a natural cause. What they are trying to hide, that Allah (God) is going to bring forth, is that there was a plan in that hospital to murder the Honorable Elijah Muhammad and he would never come out of that hospital. You damnable devils, you planned, and Allah (God) also planned.

"How did you learn this, Brother Farrakhan?" That's a good question and the answer is even better than the question. A Black man in this audience today came to me one day as I was teaching in a particular city. He was very nervous, and he said, "Brother, I have to talk to you." I told the Brother who was with me, "I cannot talk to him right now. You talk to him and see what he has to say." I got a call from him and he said,

## A Saviour is Born

"What he told me, Brother, I think it's best that you hear him out."

That man flew from where he was to where I was, visited my home. He sat down, very nervous because his life was not really clean. He knew a White woman who was one of the prostitutes who follow certain conventions. This White woman, who is alive, followed a convention to Phoenix, Arizona. They were having an orgy. Very highly placed Caucasians were involved in this orgy. They had reefer and cocaine. After the women did what they were supposed to do, they began talking.

The name of a Muslim leader came up. One of the people talking was a doctor. When this Muslim leader's name was mentioned, they said, **"We got rid of that problem nonviolently."** They all laughed. When the White woman got back to the city where the Brother was, she asked him did any Muslim leader die recently. He mentioned Malcolm X, but she said no, that wasn't the name. He said Elijah Muhammad, and she said that's the one. He was so nervous about the knowledge that he had received because the world had taken it that Elijah Muhammad just laid down and gave up the ghost from a massive congestive heart failure. But what this devil said in the room in Phoenix was, "We got rid of that problem nonviolently."

A Sister who may be in this audience tonight had the flu at that time. She was just getting over the flu and when she went to visit the Messenger, many accused that Sister of killing the Messenger because she brought a flu bug into the hospital room. In reality, it is alleged that some member or members of that staff injected it. When they are filling out a death certificate, they make it appear whatever they want it to appear. When they announced at 10 minutes after 8, some witnesses say the devil walked out and said it with a smirk on his face.

## Elijah is alive, in power

In the 4th chapter of the Qur'an, verses 157-158, it read: "And for their saying: We have killed the Messiah, Jesus, son of Mary, the messenger of Allah, and they killed him not, nor did they cause his death on the cross, but he was made to appear to them as such. And certainly those who differ therein are in doubt about it. They have no knowledge about it, but only follow a conjecture, and they killed him not for certain: Nay, Allah exalted him in His presence. And Allah is ever Mighty, Wise."

There are those attributes again: Mighty and Wise. The Honorable Elijah Muhammad said, "My mouth is not made to speak out idle words, but to speak the Will of God." Bernard Cushmeer showed me a letter that he received from the Messenger in 1966. Bernard was talking to him about the Messiah, in Daniel, that would be cut off. All the scholars admit that the cutting off means he would be without honor and respect in his own house. He would be cut off from the people. We bear witness that the Honorable Elijah Muhammad was cut off from honor and respect in his own house. He said this to Bernard Cushmeer in the letter: "It is written, Brother, that in a dark and cloudy day, the angels would come down and take him away." And he said, "smile." In the same letter, he said, "I will be delivered on the heels of a death plot."

In the history of Prophet Muhammad (PBUH), from what is called the hijirah, there was a plot against the life of Muhammad (PBUH). When they came to Muhammad's house Muhammad wasn't in the bed; Ali was in the bed. Muhammad had escaped or took flight.

During the Theology of Time lecture series, the Honorable Elijah Muhammad's wife died in 1972. He said the end would come three years after the death of the Messenger's wife. We didn't know what the end was, we thought it was the Judgment of the world. It meant the end of his first 40 days among us. He had done the job. He had paid the price and now he had to drink the bitter cup of death. But a Mighty God and a Mighty Saviour would save him from that death and confuse the enemy.

I know you think Elijah is dead. I'm here to tell you he is as alive as you are sitting right down in that seat. **Not only is he alive and well, but he is in power now.** I'm coming to you United States government. I'm coming to you Arab. I am his witness. You thought you killed him. You damnable hypocrites, you rejoiced. Now die in your rage for Elijah is back.

When Allah (God) said, *"Oh Jesus, I will cause thee to die and exalt thee in my presence and clear thee of those who disbelieve."* In another part, He says, *"I'm going to make him appear as though he were dead."* This is God's plan overlaying the Jews' plans, overlaying the Arabs' plan, overlaying the government's plans. He's making all their plans to serve His plan. "Where is your proof, Farrakhan?"

## A Saviour is Born

First, the Honorable Elijah Muhammad told us, "If Allah (God) had not shown him how he was going to escape, he would have no hope at all." One day at the table, he was talking on the finality of death. His son was at the table, one of the good ones. His son was questioning him. "Daddy, you mean that when we die, we can never be brought back." He said, "That's right, son."

His son kept pressing him, and then he said, "Well, if he's a real great man and Allah (God) favors him much, if Allah (God) gets the body within 24 hours, He can revive him." We live in a world where you die and have out-of-body experiences, but the White man, even with his limited knowledge, can bring you back. Some scholars feel that the body of Jesus was switched. It is written in the footnotes of the Qur'an.

Here's a challenge. If Elijah Muhammad lies dead in that grave, bring the body up. Since the family exhumed it once, and kept it locked in a room in the temple, with a guard being paid a salary, armed just to protect a dead body for over a year. Then they "reburied" him.

Among the Bilalian Muslims, there is a doctor who worked on the Messenger's teeth. He has the records. Exhume the body and prove me a liar. Go get the dental records and match it with the teeth of the one you think you buried. You go and do that.

I am here to tell you: He is risen. I am here to tell you, that one, the Jesus that you've been looking for has been in your midst for 40 years and you didn't recognize him. He is styled under the Holy Ghost because of the darkness of your and my ignorance. A Holy One was working among us, and we didn't know who he was until after he was gone.

## The resurrection of faith

When he was gone, we fell apart. I, Louis Farrakhan, was one of those who was like Peter, that

## A Saviour is Born

strong witness of the Lord. But my faith hadn't grown yet to be what it should have been. Therefore, my faith failed me, not altogether.

The Honorable Elijah Muhammad looked me straight in my face and I was too dumb to pick up, when he said, "Brother, I tell you like Jesus said to Peter, the devil desires you that he may sift you as wheat." (Luke 22:31) The following verse (32) reads, "but I have prayed for you, that your faith may not fail you altogether. And when you have returned to me, go and strengthen your brethren." I am telling you that this is the Peter that you have been reading about all of the days of your life. Take it or let it alone. Elijah Muhammad is the Christ that you hope for.

My faith failed. I know some of you are shocked like h---. Just like the scripture says, "Before the cock crows once, Peter, you will deny me thrice." It was 30 months exactly that I was a Bilalian, trying to harmonize Wallace's teaching with his father's. Thirty long months in agony. Thirty months in the grave. Thirty months dead. The world witnessed me die. The world witnessed a nation die.

The Messenger said to me, "Brother don't you change the Teachings while I'm gone." He said, "I'll be gone approximately three years." There's a lot of wisdom and science in that. "Now, Brother," he says, "what I've given you is just a wake-up message. But if you are faithful, when I return"—that's right, not *"if"*—*"when* I return, I will reveal the new teaching through you."

The Messenger told us a new book was coming. We are about to walk straight out of the Holy Qur'an. We are about to fulfill the Holy Qur'an. Do you wonder at this announcement? My 30 months with Wallace D. Mohammed was preparation for me. He was to be to me like Satan is to us as a nation. to sift me like wheat. I don't have time to go into all of that, but I was thoroughly sifted.

## A Saviour is Born

The Messenger said, "Now, Brother, the same power that is with me will be with you. In fact, about it, there will be two of us backing you up—Allah (God) and myself." He said, "Brother, anything that you want, ask Allah (God) in my name and He will give it to you."

I'm listening to him. This is in 1974, but I don't fully understand. All I said was, "yes, sir." He said, "I'll be gone approximately three years." He's right. I was gone, but when I came back to him, he came back to me. What you have been listening to all over this country for the last three-and-a-half years—40 to 41 months, you have the same preparation in his beginning, now there's 40 to 41 months again in this new beginning—you've been listening to the voice of the Messenger.

I, Farrakhan, don't have any power to give life. The voice of Elijah coming through me is giving life now to a nation. When you turn me down, you are

## A Saviour is Born

turning down the Lord that you say you seek. After the tomb was opened, they didn't see him as he was; they saw him as gardener. He's working in the garden, plucking up weeds, separating wheat from tare.

You may laugh at this announcement, and you may mock but the Messenger told all his followers and you and the world. Look and listen. What you see done, even though you look at it, you're not going to believe it. I'm telling you that our Father is in heaven. "What do you mean heaven? Is he floating up?" No, come on now. We don't believe in anything spooky. He's alive. He and The God are together. His return is imminent.

The Messenger kept saying before, that Allah (God) would destroy the devil. But as we got closer to the time that he was to leave us, he said, "I will destroy this devil." He said Jehovah gave Moses the power, with the rod that he had, to destroy Pharoah.

One of your Brothers has been exalted to the position of the right hand of God. One of your

## A Saviour is Born

Brothers has been given by the Lord of the Worlds the power to control the forces of nature. That's why the Honorable Elijah Muhammad asks us in the Student Enrollment, "who is" not "who was" the Original Man. He said, "I am the Original Man."

I am the Owner, and I am the Maker. I'm the Cream of the Planet and I'm now the God of the Universe. If he's not God, you can't be. If he's not resurrected, you can't rise. If he's not raised from the dead, then there's no hope of us ever being raised.

I came back. I was dead, not totally, partially. People looked at Farrakhan and said, "That n----- is gone." Some of the Bilalians who wanted to kill me, I was so pitiful, they said there's no use in killing him; he's already dead.

Look at the wise way God and the Messenger guided the rebuilding of the Nation of Islam. That's not Farrakhan. That's Elijah. That's God present with us. Look at these clean Brothers. Look at their faces.

Don't they look like the old soldiers of Muhammad. Who raised them up? Who made these men? It's Muhammad who raised them. Who put the Sisters back in their white robes? It's Muhammad who did that. Who lifted the flag up again? It's Muhammad who did that, Brothers and Sisters.

## Warning to hypocrites and enemies

In my conclusion and a warning to the hypocrites: You have just a few days to come back to yourself, or the Chastisement of Allah (God) will overtake you this year.

To the Arabs and the whole Muslim world—you delight yourself in saying that we are not true Muslims. To the whole Muslim world: You are not true Muslims. If you don't reason with this resurrection that is taking place, after you, Arabs, helped to sell our fathers into slavery. You joined trade in Black bodies. After we were brought into bondage, 400 years later,

## A Saviour is Born

God gives us a deliverer, and you conspire, Arab, with the government of oppression to destroy our deliverer.

To the Arab world: Your destruction has now entered your door. Unless you come and bear witness and bow down—mark the words of a servant of the Honorable Elijah Muhammad—the Arab world will be bathed in blood.

You devils, the government of the United States of America, we are raised up again as a dare. Our Father and His God dare you to touch us. It may be that to prove he is with us, within three months a major calamity will strike America to prove to the government of America, that we are no longer a forsaken people, but that God is present and with us.

For those of you who think this is a little pushover, then gather all that you have and come against us and give us no respite, as the Qur'an teaches. Allah (God) will slay you all either by our hands or by His Almighty Hand.

### A Saviour is Born

To Mr. Reagan, I am a reminder to you, Mr. Reagan, of the warning of the Honorable Elijah Muhammad that the Black man in America is to be separated from you and is to go free, or America is to be destroyed.

Reagan has the power to delay the judgement; he can't do away with it, but he can delay it. In order for Mr. Reagan to delay the judgement, he must study Abraham Lincoln, and give reparations to the Black man and woman of America for 400 years of our undeserved suffering, trial, and tribulation.

Are you happy, White folks, over your hostages that have been released after 444 days? What about 30 million hostages who have been held here against their will for 400 years? This is your last chance, America.

The FBI that is present here today, the CIA that is present here today, take this message back to your field office and to Washington. This that you see budding here in America, we have determined that this

Nation will never go down again. We have determined that you will have to kill us all—men, women, and children. We have determined that our people are going to be free. We have determined, as the Bible says, he will send saviours—plural—after them.

Every one of us who has a knowledge of God and a knowledge of the truth, we have a responsibility to go after our people to save them from the Wrath of God that is coming down on America.

**Muslim Fight Song**

I leave you, my beloved Black Brothers and Sisters, my Muslim Brothers and Sisters, especially the older Muslims—you have paid a tremendous price to bring about the new rise of the Nation. Don't feel bad about yesterday.

It was absolutely necessary to produce in you and me the growth into the Messenger, that we would not just know him, but we would act on his words.

## A Saviour is Born

Brother William 12X, here's a Brother—please bring him out front. The police attacked the temple in 1962 on unarmed Muslims and they were shot down. This Brother lost the use of his limbs. He paid a price. We paid a price.

To think that the enemy of the Messenger would make a Brother, who paid a price like this, believe that his Messenger lied and that his suffering was all in vain. Brother William, look at a new nation coming up in front of you. Know that your pain and suffering, undeserved, is responsible for bringing up a new nation and new generation of Muslims.

So, lift your head up and never look down. Be willing, not only to lose our limbs, but to lose our lives for the redemption of all our people. May Allah (God) bless you. May Allah (God) keep you. May Allah (God) lift up His countenance upon you, Black man and woman. You are the choice of God. You are the people of the Christ. You are destined to rule.

A Saviour is Born

*[singing the "Muslim Fight Song" of the Nation of Islam]*

We are fighting for Islam and we will surely win.
With our Saviour, Allah, The Universal King.
We are united with our Nation and called by His Name.
So let us rise, ye Muslims. Fight for your own.
Fight oh ye Muslims, fight for your own.
Fight for your Nation and we will all be free.
Fight for your Nation. Fight for your own.

Freedom, Justice, and Equality, we now must have.
400 years a slave for devils, lost from our own.
So let us rise, ye Muslims. Fight for your own.
Fight o ye Muslims, fight for your own.
Fight for your Nation and we will all be free.
Fight for your Nation. Fight for your own.

The earth belongs to the righteous. Fight for your own.
Allah gave you and I for a national: the sun, the moon, the star.
The best of His creation, He has given to you.
So let us rise, ye Muslims. Fight for your own.
Fight o ye Muslims. Fight for your own.
Fight for your Nation and we will all be free.
Fight for your Nation. Fight for your own.

(whisper)
The earth belongs to the righteous. Fight for your own.
Allah gave you and I for a national: the sun, the moon, the star.
The best of His creation, He has given to you.
So let us rise, ye Muslims. Fight for your own.
Fight o ye Muslims. Fight for your own.
Fight for your Nation and we will all be free.
Fight for your Nation. Fight for your own.

## Rebirth of a Nation

All praise is due to Allah (God). We now have something to fight for, we have our own to fight for. We want to let the world know we intend to fight like h--- for our own.

If there are no more announcements—Brothers and Sisters, keep standing. There's been an acceptance card put in your seat along with this folder. If you would like to become a part of this Nation and worldwide movement, fill out your name, pass in that card and you will be hearing from us. Today's lecture is on tape, and you can get it right now on your way out. If you would like to purchase a souvenir's journal of today's historic Rebirth of a Nation, it also is on sale on your way out.

All of the Messenger's books. "Message to the Black Man in America"—don't leave home without it. "Our Saviour Has Arrived"—go home with it. And look at your Brother—in a few days I will be 50 years

## A Saviour is Born

old; not a few days, about a year-and-a-half. I look pretty good for a man who is middle-aged. How do we shine like this, Brothers? We're eating better. We're living better. You ought to get this book, "How to Eat to Live." In fact, many of us eat now, every other day. Most of the Muslims eat once a day. The Honorable Elijah Muhammad told me he wanted me to eat twice a week. That's alright, I may be invisible, but I'll be here. Brother and Sister, I know it sounds far-fetched, but let me tell you. If you start eating one meal a day, get that nasty pig off your table, hog maw, chitterlings, and fatback, and all that bad food out of your refrigerator, and put good wholesome, healthy, clean food, you will live a longer life. This is on sale on the way out.

There's a little booklet by Sister Tynnetta Muhammad on the woman in Islam, dealing with the beginning of the study of the domestic life of the Honorable Elijah Muhammad. You need to get this,

## A Saviour is Born

take it home, and study it. It's on sale for a minimum cost. Last, but not least, here is a record album of a song I recorded in 1956 called, "A White man's heaven is a Black man's hell." I rerecorded it in May of 1980, with strings and great Black musicians. There is a speech on here given to all the disk jockeys and record personalities in Atlanta, Georgia. So, it's a two-record album. It's on sale. You can get it on your way out. Everything that you buy, the proceeds will help us to rebuild the Nation of Islam.

Tonight, across the street, we're going to have the conclusion of this wonderful convention, a Saviours' Day dinner. You should get a seat and eat dinner. Naturally, it costs money but let's be together. Then, let us go back to our cities, Muslims, and double, triple, and quadruple our efforts so that next year this time, there will be 10,000 strong—and you know what happened when Muhammad (PBUH) came back to Mecca with 10,000. Will you pray with us?

# ABOUT THE FINAL CALL FOUNDATION

The Final Call Foundation was established in 2021 with the purpose to support raising awareness, preserving, researching, and amplifying the public works and personal history of the Honorable Minister Louis Farrakhan in the uplift of all humanity.

Follow us:  @finalcallfoundation
@FCFcharity

Visit The Final Call Foundation Amazon Author Page for release updates

## **<u>Upcoming Title</u>**

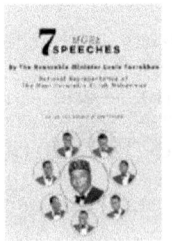

**7 More Speeches** by the Honorable Minister Louis Farrakhan

*On the Sacredness of The Female*

## Available Titles

**Sarah:** Five Notes on a Woman's Prayer over Her Pregnancy
*A Study of the Biblical Matriarch of the Children of Israel and Mother Sumayyah Farrakhan of the Nation of Islam*

**A Demonstration of Love**
*A special collection of articles and editorials*

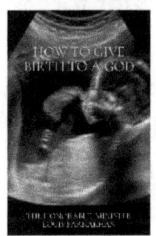

**How To Give Birth To A God**
by the Honorable Minister Louis Farrakhan

**A Reason to Unite**
Hurricane Katrina and the Millions More Movement by the Honorable Minister Louis Farrakhan

## ABOUT THE EDITOR

Dora Muhammad is an artist, author, and advocate. She served as editor-in-chief of *The Final Call* Newspaper from 2003-2006. In 2010, she founded The AWARE Project, a multimedia vehicle for advocacy on issues relative to women's awareness, engagement, rights, empowerment, and advancement. She earned a Bachelor of Arts in Journalism and Documentary Photography, with a concentration in Magazine Production and completed her photography thesis at Dartington School of the Arts in Devon, England. She worked as an arts administrator for Autograph-ABP (Association of Black Photographers) while studying International Law and Human Rights at the University of London. Dora earned her Master of Public Administration and has extensive work in government relations and public policy formation. A daughter of Indo-Caribbean immigrant parents, Dora is a native New Yorker who resides in Northern Virginia. She currently serves as the executive director of The Final Call Foundation.

Visit the Dora Muhammad and AWARE Project Amazon Author Pages for a catalog of her books.

www.ingramcontent.com/pod-product-compliance
Lightning Source LLC
Chambersburg PA
CBHW060201050426
42446CB00013B/2941